TEXAS DISASTER LAW GUIDE

Legal Considerations for Emergency Responders and Managers

TEXAS DISASTER LAW GUIDE

Legal Considerations for Emergency Responders and Managers

Edited by Alfonso López de la Osa Escribano,
Tracy Hester and Bryan Sky-Eagle

Arte Público Press
Houston, Texas

Publication of *Texas Disaster Law Guide: Legal Considerations for Emergency Responders and Managers* is made possible with support from Rice University's Baker Institute Center for the United States and Mexico, the Center for US and Mexican Law at the University of Houston Law Center, Texas OneGulf Center of Excellence, the Mission Foods Texas-Mexico Center at Southern Methodist University, the Facultad de Derecho y Criminología at the Universidad Autónoma de Nuevo León, the Escuela de Gobierno y Transformación Pública at the Tecnológico de Monterrey and the Departamento de Estudios Internacionales of the Universidad Iberoamericana.

Recovering the past, creating the future

Arte Público Press
University of Houston
4902 Gulf Freeway, Bldg 19, Rm 100
Houston, Texas 77204-2004

Cover design by Mora Des¡gn
Cover photos used with permission from the Houston Chronicle.
Cover photo by Karen Warren/©Houston Chronicle.
Cover photo by Melissa Phillip/©Houston Chronicle.

TABLE OF CONTENTS

Appendix A: Field Guidebook Flowcharts

Appendix B: Sample EOC Skillset

ACKNOWLEDGEMENTS

The Texas OneGulf Center of Excellence partners would like to thank the following scholars and faculty for their research and preparation of this report:

Bryan Sky-Eagle, JD, CFO
Affiliate Scholar, Center for U.S. and Mexican Law
University of Houston Law Center
District Chief of the Houston Fire Department

Dr. Alfonso López de la Osa Escribano, PhD, JD, LLM
Director, Center for U.S. and Mexican Law
Adjunct Faculty
University of Houston Law Center

Tracy Hester, JD, BA
Associate Instructional Professor
University of Houston Law Center
Co-Director and Co-Founder of the
Center for Carbon Management in Energy
University of Houston

The present analysis is part of the research project: "RESTORE Centers of Excellence: Hurricane Harvey Decision-Support-Resilient Environments and Communities (1RCEGR480001/TCEQ 582-15-57594/GAD 91613)" 2018-2020.

This project was paid for [in part] with federal funding from the Department of the Treasury through the State of Texas under the Resources and Ecosystems Sustainability, Tourist Opportunities, and Revived Economies of the Gulf Coast States Act of 2012 (RESTORE Act).

Texas OneGulf is a RESTORE funded consortium of nine top state institutions led by the Harte Research Institute (HRI) for Gulf of Mexico Studies at Texas A&M University-Corpus Christi with wide-ranging expertise in the environment, the economy, and human health. This project was paid for with grant funding from the Texas OneGulf Center of Excellence. The content, statements, findings, opinions, and recommendations are those of the authors and do not necessarily reflect the views of the Texas OneGulf Center of Excellence, the HARTE Research Institute, or the Center for the U.S. and Mexican Law at the University of Houston Law Center. Copyright © 2020.

FOREWORD

The significance and complexity of disasters, as well as the urgency of building resilience to those disasters, cannot be overstated. As I write this in the United States in Fall 2020, the COVID-19 pandemic continues to devastate communities as a health and economic crisis, wildfires are scorching land and cities in the west with a mounting death toll, western Louisiana is only beginning to think about rebuilding after clearing out the destruction caused by Hurricane Laura, Hurricane Sally formed and is headed to northern Gulf shores, and for only the second time in history there are five active tropical cyclones in the Atlantic.

Yet, as we strive to confront the challenges of today, so too must we continue to address remaining and systemic challenges from our past that continue to obfuscate our ability to derive solutions. With winds in excess of 130 mph, Hurricane Harvey made landfall in Rockport and Fulton, South Texas as a Category 4 storm on August 25, 2017. In the initial impact and torrential rain of the ensuing days, Harvey caused widespread destruction along the Texas coast, resulting in 103 confirmed US deaths and an estimated $125 billion in damages—the second costliest hurricane ever, following Katrina. Three years later, Texas communities are still struggling to build back stronger, more resilient communities along the coast—communities that can better withstand the impacts of future events, and that are positioned to make a 'developmental leap' by mitigating risk while aligning growth with recovery efforts, all while simultaneously striving, against great adversity, to meet the demands of today.

The framework offered herein provides a beacon of light in a key but oft-obscured area of resilience, the legal considerations emergency responders and managers face when dealing with natural disasters. As we learned in Hurricane Harvey, it is vital that our first responders have crystal clear understanding and guidance on the extent of their authority to protect life and property. However, every disaster is unique, and too often our first line of defense—the very people we rely on to keep us safe in times of crisis—themselves are left to clarify complex legal concepts in urgent situations. From which rules or laws are suspended in times of disaster, to who may request and provide mutual aid assistance, to risk and liability in an emergency response and more, Texas first responders need answers. This framework, crafted carefully with input from local emergency personnel as well as the Texas Division of Emergency Management, makes great strides toward enhancing the understanding needed to make tough calls in seemingly impossible times.

Notably, this project was supported by the Texas OneGulf Center of Excellence, a RESTORE Act funded consortium of nine top state institutions led by the Harte Research Institute (HRI) for Gulf of Mexico Studies at Texas A&M University-Corpus Christi with wide-ranging expertise in the environment, the economy and human health. The interdisciplinary project sought to better understand and offer recommendations on how Texas can help its environment, communities and social systems better rebound from Harvey. We are encouraged to offer this important work as a practical asset to Texas communities in strengthening their response and recovery frameworks, and look forward to continuing our partnerships to build a resilient Texas and Gulf.

Dr. Katya Wowk
Director
Texas OneGulf Center of Excellence

PREFACE

Natural disasters seem to be increasing nowadays on the planet. Texas is well situated to talk about it due to the number of hurricanes that recurrently impact the Lone Star state. The approach from decision-makers, first responders and the community has moved from real-time reactions to try to cope with the situation in the best way possible, towards prevention and preparedness, improving actions to face disasters by conceiving different possible scenarios and solutions in advance.

One might use different terms to denominate this new field of law that deals with disasters response and prevention: *Disasters Law*, *Disasters Recovery Law*, *Disasters Risk Reduction*, *Disasters and Resilience Law*, *Natural Disasters Management and Resilience Law*, among others. All of them want to witness the relevance of the law in dealing with understanding how to mitigate what traditionally has been called *Acts of God*, where communities were driven back to a stoic *fatum* resignation. The need to structure into a legal framework the capacity communities have to respond to natural or human-made disasters is critical today. The law regulates society. The law structures and responds to society's needs and fulfills the gaps existing. Not only do we have to resist, we also need to cope with the situation and be well prepared. We need to be resilient.

Through resilience we understand the human capacity to adapt with extreme flexibility to situations in order to overcome them. From an even more human psychological dimension, we may add too, the way traumatic situations make someone stronger. Resilience implies we rethink positions to imagine new solutions, to be prepared for similar scenarios in the future. Due to the intensity of climate disasters we unfortunately know in advance that those situations will happen again. Not only are resilient communities ready to overcome adversity, but disaster makes them grow stronger and reach their maximum resilient potential, as would a reborn Ave Phoenix. We never choose a natural catastrophe, but our self-determination to overcome it is critical. The impact caused by a natural disaster such as Hurricane Harvey in Texas, is tough to live through; it is traumatic from a human perspective. A resilient community empathetically and positively looks ahead while minimizing the real-time cost of human suffering, trying to get back to everyday life when possible, the sooner the better. Beneath Disasters Risk or Natural

Disasters and Response Law lies the humanistic dimension of the law, its inherent principle of protecting human lives and our community. Without this dimension, the law becomes null.

When setting a common legal framework for Disaster Risk Management, it is necessary to identify standard rules and see how the existing mechanisms can be improved where deficiencies exist. Without any doubt, the law has become a tool for disaster mitigation; moreover, when we need to manage society and the materialization and manifestation of natural disasters, their risks become a more recurrent matter.

The reflection on the research performed for this book has been very stimulating. The purpose of this handbook is to provide answers about the legal considerations emergency responders and managers should face when dealing with natural disasters and by analogy, to catastrophic situations.

We hope readers will find the answers they are looking for. From the Center for US and Mexican Law at the University of Houston Law Center and as part of the Texas One Gulf Consortium, we would like to bring our perspective to the discussion. It is essential to shed light on many of the legal circumstances that may turn up when seeking solutions and making decisions in real-time disasters response.

Alfonso López de la Osa Escribano
Principal Investigator
Director, Center for U.S. and Mexican Law
University of Houston Law Center

EXECUTIVE SUMMARY
OBJECTIVES & METHODOLOGY

After Hurricane Harvey decimated the Texas coast in 2017, the Center for U.S. and Mexican Law at the University of Houston Law Center initiated a series of interviews with first responders and public stakeholders to further understand and improve disaster response. The Center for U.S. and Mexican Law is part of the Texas OneGulf Consortium project with the Harte Research Institute and within the research project 'RESTORE Centers of Excellence: Hurricane Harvey Decision—Support—Resilient Environments and Communities.' From this effort, various professional disciplines expressed common concerns that gave rise to the content of this book. Subsequent hazardous material fires and chemical spills in the Texas water channels and coastal areas, along with the evolving effects of climate change, demonstrate that these natural and man-made disasters have begun to expand the boundaries of disaster law, justifying a more in-depth analysis of this new branch of the law. Disaster Law arises from the lessons learned from past catastrophes, and this can shape the critical and irreversible decisions made by those in charge of response efforts during the response phase of a disaster. Texas communities are subject to federal, state and local laws that address emergency and disaster response, and the fact that first responders and emergency managers will be called upon to carry out those laws is undeniable. Their knowledge is, therefore, essential today. The core legal issues related to the response phase include, but are not limited to:

- Public authorities for emergency response
- Modifications of the scope of employment
- Liability of responders
- Suspension of relevant laws during a state of a declared emergency

The purpose of this framework is to give answers about the legal considerations emergency responders and managers should face when dealing with natural disasters and catastrophic situations. The framework also provides high priority recommendations to state and local decision-makers in strengthening Texas' resilience.

While this framework has an expansive scope, it focuses on the policy and legal considerations in declared emergencies and the decisions taken in this context. Notably, however, its content only represents a sample of the laws and policies that disaster response can invoke and aims primarily at state laws and policies, although it also discusses some local provisions in specific examples. It is also important to note that Texas allows the governor or mayor to suspend laws during times of disaster response, which would not apply to this framework.[1] Several questions come to mind when identifying the purpose of the present framework. These are the questions we will seek to answer: Is there an international background for disaster law framework? Is there any impact of those recommendations in Texas Law? From the strategic level (the City council), going through the tactical level (Fire Chief departments), and ending up at the task level (First responders), what are the elements to keep in mind when making a decision where time is of the essence? What are the legal issues around those situations? What should lead the decision when there would be a lack of a law to be applied? What are the needed ethical aspects of the decision? What do we seek to achieve? Can reasonable or compelling force be used? When? How can risk be minimized? Why is training and education in managing emergency response critical? Why are communication techniques so critical?

This project identifies and analyzes the legal issues that affect first responders, emergency managers and other response providers during the response phase of a disaster. It offers its conclusions in a format designed to assist Texas agencies and communities in their efforts to navigate relevant laws and policies of disaster response.

First Responder Terminology & Field Guidebook Flowcharts

Merriam-Wester dictionary defines a first responder as "a person (such as a police officer or an Emergency Medical Technician-EMT) who is among those responsible for going immediately to the scene of an accident or an emergency to assist."[2] This description seems to reflect the public's understanding when referring to first responders, but this can also apply to dozens of other professions.[3] Likewise, multitudes of laws refer to, or scarcely define "the first responder," but their usage lies well beyond the scope of this framework. This framework, recognizing the expanding field, focuses on government responders but may also pertain to private responsible parties and non-governmental or quasi-governmental agencies. To make information usable in field operations we provide sample flowcharts in Appendix A. The flowcharts can be reduced to a pocket-sized guide for responders, commanders and emergency managers during deployment to remote command posts or operations centers.

Endnotes

[1]Tex. Gov't Code § 418.016(a).
[2]http://www.merriam-webster.com/dictionary/first%20responder.
[3]http://www.usfra.org/notes/Who_is_a _First_Responder?show=true.

INTRODUCTION
LAW & DISASTER RESPONSE & RESILIENCE
PROJECT BACKGROUND

In March 2015, the United Nations (UN) adopted the *Sendai Framework for Disaster Risk Reduction 2015-2030*, after a process of consultation with stakeholders and governments that started in 2012.[1] This instrument is considered the second act of United Nations actions after the *Hyogo Framework for Action (HFA) 2005-2015: Building Resilience of Nations and Communities to Disasters*. Moving from disaster management to disaster risk management, the Sendai Framework seeks to define several global targets, preventing new risks, reducing the existing ones and bringing resilience to a superior level by understanding disaster risks, vulnerability and hazards, strengthening disaster risk governance and accountability for disaster risk management.[2]

While we achieved progress in building resilience and reducing damages, we need to do more, focusing primarily on people and their health, preventing and reducing hazard exposure and vulnerability to disaster, increasing preparedness to react, to respond and to recover with the correspondent impact on resilience. For that, a broader involvement of political leadership is required at all levels, internationally, nationally and locally. To achieve this outcome, the Sendai Framework enumerates the multi-factorial dimension of the measures whose adoption grants an integrated perspective: economic, structural, legal, social, health, cultural, educational, environmental, technological, political and institutional.[3] The purpose of the present framework and research under the Texas OneGulf Consortium Project is situated in the legal dimension of disaster risk reduction and management and could not be more timely.

1. The Sendai Global targets

The *Sendai Framework for Disaster Risk Reduction* agreed on seven global targets (along with four priority areas[4]) that allow measurement of the achievements of outcomes set by the UN instrument, serving as an inspiration, among others, to the legislative production in the respective country dealing with disaster risk management and response. The seven global targets set by the Sendai Framework are:[5]

    a. To reduce **global disaster mortality** by 2030, lowering the average per 100,000 global mortality rate between 2020 and 2030, compared to the period 2005-2015.

b. To reduce the number of **affected people globally** by 2030, reducing the global figure per 100,000 between 2020 and 2030, compared to the period 2005-2015.
c. To reduce **disaster economic loss related to GDP** (Global gross domestic product) by 2030.
d. To reduce **disaster damage to crucial infrastructure and disruption of essential services** (i.e., health and educational facilities), making them more resilient by 2030.
e. To increase the **number of countries that have a national and local disaster risk reduction strategy** by 2020.
f. To enhance **international cooperation in developing countries** through adequate and sustainable support to complement their national actions by 2030.
g. To increase access **to multi-hazard early warning systems and disaster risk information and assessments** to people by 2030.

2. Understanding disaster risk

Disaster risk is defined by the Sendai Framework as the way to understand the vulnerabilities, capacities and exposure of the persons and assets involved, in order to know the hazard characteristics and analyze the situation and evolution of the environment. Knowledge is critical to evaluate in advance of risk of a probable natural disaster in order to prevent and mitigate it and to develop and implement preparedness and effective response to disasters.[6] The collection of data and practical information, as well as to dissociate any private protected information before disseminating it, are part of how authorities need to understand risk. The generation of this knowledge is what allows decision-makers to address community needs. This information should be readily available and accessible in real-time by everyone.

By understanding risk, we consider the periodic assessment of vulnerability, capacity and exposure of communities, including risk maps that need to be known by decision-makers and the public, especially by those communities that are more exposed than others. Information and communication technologies can be a way to measure, collect and analyze data (surveys; disaster risk modeling; assessment; mapping; monitoring; multi-hazard warning systems). Generating awareness and building knowledge at all levels of society is essential.

From a multi-factorial dimension, to understand disaster risk management also goes through the promotion of dialogue and cooperation between scientific and technological communities, relevant stakeholders and policymakers to facilitate a scientific interface for effective decision-making on disaster risk management. This cooperation also goes through the combination of different types of knowledge (traditional, indigenous, local, scientific) to develop policies, strategies, plans and programs for specific sectors. One need to consider disaster prevention, mitigation, preparedness, response, recovery and rehabilitation as well, by promoting a culture of disaster resilience.

3. Strengthening disaster risk governance and responsibility of states to prevent and reduce disaster risk

One of the guiding principles set by the Sendai Framework highlights that each state's primary responsibility is to prevent and reduce disaster risk, including through cooperation. Disaster risk reduction requires that between the central government, local government and relevant national authorities and stakeholders share overall responsibilities and authorities to protect persons, properties and health. Institutional integrated engagement means to work through partnership and from an inclusive point of view to avoid discrimination, specifically from those strongly affected by the disaster, and among others, the poor. Also, to manage and reduce disaster risk, coordination of relevant stakeholders at all levels and the total engagement of the Nation's institutions is promoted.[7] From executive and legislative institutions at the national level to those at local levels. We consider that the University or business sectors also need to articulate responsibilities through the public and private sectors to obtain the mutual outreach sought. The United Nations Office for Disaster Risk Reduction (UNDRR) acknowledges the existence of gaps in a public and private partnership that exist when addressing disaster risk reduction management, including gaps in urban planning and environmental laws associated with buildings' safety, land use by constructors and spatial planning by public authorities. That is why a coherent, inclusive and robust legal framework is a critical tool for good governance in order to reduce the risks that may be caused by natural disasters and in order not to create more risks by human decisions of urban planning.

Society is interlinked and interconnected when addressing disaster risk management. Private sectors must also seek solutions to mitigate risks connected to natural disasters and bring solutions from a shared responsibility perspective. Every action, public or private investment, should be risk-informed, including in standard market mechanisms. By doing so, societies will reduce risks by creating strategies that foster resilient communities.[8]

The Federal governments will exert the role of coordinator at the national level, and at the same time, local authorities and communities have to be empowered to reduce disaster risk. This empowerment can be done by providing resources, incentives and identifying decision-making responsibilities. While disaster risk can be analyzed through a global perspective, reducing it requires an understanding of locally specific characteristics. This empowerment can deal with a lack of understanding and communication that exists in these situations. Further, policies, plans, practices or mechanisms can target coherence among the many various factors involved, such as growth and sustainable development, food security, health and safety, climate change, environmental management and disaster risk reduction agendas.

While legislation may be pertinent to and envision precise situations, there is sometimes a gap or distance between the enacted legislation and the specific implementation and enforcement of those norms. The lack of resources at the local level, the weak culture of compliance or the fact that local governments are not prioritizing disaster risk reduction may be among the causes of this lack of correlation.[9] We need to empower local authorities through regulatory and financial tools to work and coordinate with society in ways to manage disaster risk at the local level.

By strengthening disaster risk governance the Sendai Framework considers the creation of effective and efficient mechanisms of disaster risk management (*clear vision plans, competence, guidance and coordination across sectors and participation of relevant stakeholders*).[10] It is relevant to promote and develop a coherent national and local set of laws, regulations and public policies that define responsibilities and roles, promote incentives for the community, enhance transparency, financial incentives and awareness and create organizational structures, to achieve this goal. Good governance also includes the promotion of public analysis and encouragement of institutional debates. Legislators should amend relevant legislation and allocate budgets. Those mechanisms should ensure compliance with safety provisions considered in laws and regulations (such as mentioned, land use, urban planning, building codes, environmental, health and safety standards). Also, when formulating public policies, aspects such as prevention or relocations of persons and human settlements in disaster zones should be taken into account.

4. Preparedness to build back better

Another interesting priority is to further strengthen disaster preparedness in order to respond to and take actions in an anticipated way, combining both disaster risk reduction (taking steps in advance to avoid the situation if possible) and building the capacities and effective response at every level of the decision-making and action chain. Interestingly, the Sendai Framework highlights equality and inclusiveness, empowering women and persons with disabilities with an equitable and universally accessible response, recovery, rehabilitation and reconstruction phase.[11] We need to prepare recovery, rehabilitation and reconstruction phases in advance, following the notion the Sendai Framework calls "Build Back Better."

At national and state levels, we need to accomplish several actions in order to achieve this "Build Back Better" priority. It may serve as a recommendation to develop an appropriate set of rules in order to anticipate the adversity of climate disasters with equity in mind. By achieving resilience and "Build Back Better," we also understand to review regular plans and programs seeking to consider the different situations that can happen and their impact. We can develop early warning plans and systems, encouraging the participation of all actors. Among these actors we should involve infrastructure experts to grant the resilience of buildings, telecommunications and transportation infrastructures, grid[12] and hospitals, among others.

Other actions that allow us to achieve resilience to train first responders, workforce and voluntary forces in coordinated disaster response exercises, including evacuations, relocations, access to safe shelters or to provide food. Let us turn to this now.

Endnotes

[1]Sendai Framework for Disaster Risk Reduction 2015-2030, allows us to globally agree and understand disaster risk management and mitigation, from an innovative implementation perspective by taking into account holistically the different sectors prevention and preparedness that need to be taken into account. Sendai Framework for Disaster Risk Reduction 2015-2030, United Nations (accessed December 15, 2019).

[2]Cfr. Foreword, Margareta Wahlstrom, United Nations Special Representative of the Secretary General for Disaster Risk Reduction, *ibidem*.

[3]*Ibidem*, Paragraph 17.

[4]Understanding disaster risk; Strengthening disaster risk governance to manage disaster risk; Investing in disaster risk reduction for resilience; Enhancing disaster preparedness for effective response and to "Build Back Better" in recovery, rehabilitation and reconstruction. Cfr. Sendai Framework for Disaster Risk Reduction 2015-2030, United Nations, IV Priorities for Action, Paragraph 20 (*accessed December 15, 2019*).

[5]*Ibidem*, Paragraph 18.

[6]Cfr. *Ibidem*, Priority 1. Paragraph 23.

[7]Cfr. *Ibidem*, *Guiding Principles.* Paragraph (e).

[8]K.L.H. Samuel, M. Aronsson-Storrier, K. Nakjavani Bookmiller, *The Cambridge Handbook of Disaster Risk Reduction and International Law,* Cambridge University Press, 2019, Foreword by Paola Albrito, p. xvi.

[9]K.L.H. Samuel, M. Aronsson-Storrier, K. Nakjavani Bookmiller, *The Cambridge Handbook of Disaster Risk Reduction and International Law,* Cambridge University Press, 2019, Foreword by Paola Albrito, p. xv.

[10]Cfr. Sendai Framework for Disaster Risk Reduction 2015-2030, United Nations, IV Priorities for Action, Paragraph 26 (*accessed December 15, 2019*).

[11]To know more about equality and natural disasters, cfr. Kristina Cedervall Lauta, "Human rights and natural disasters," *Research Handbook on Disasters and International Law,* Edward Elgar Publishing, 2016, p. 91.

[12]To know more about building resilient grid, see Rosemary Lyster and Robert R.M. Verchick, "Protecting the power grid from climate disasters," *Research Handbook on Climate Disaster Law, Barriers and Opportunities,* Edward Elgar Publishing, 2018, p. 275.

PART 1

DISASTER
RESPONSE LAW

A mandatory evacuation occurs when emergency management officials order a compulsory evacuation in a particular area as a protective action to save the lives of the persons in the area: residents, passersby and first responders. In Texas, a county judge or mayor of a municipality who orders an evacuation may compel persons who remain in the evacuated area to leave and they can authorize the use of reasonable force to remove such persons.[1] While this legal power places great weight on the exact threshold under which force remains "reasonable," the statute does not define the terms "reasonable force" and "compel." As a result, the responsible elected official retains a great degree of discretion to determine the scale of a mandatory evacuation. First responders should also note that the issuance of such orders can trigger other individual constitutional rights and require the government to provide additional services to carry out a mandatory evacuation (i.e., transportation). With this backdrop, first responders do not have much guidance on determining the correct level of force to execute the evacuation order and may want to contact legal counsel.

Example of Evacuation Reasonable Force

During Hurricane Harvey, disaster response officials cut electrical power to flooded homes which deterred people from returning to inundated areas. This action avoided emergency responders being dispatched to dangerous flooded locations which posed threats of electrocution and structure fires.

"Mandatory evacuation issued for flooded homes near Addicks and Barker reservoirs." ABC13.com. Retrieved from https://abc13.com/power-cut-to-flooded-homes-in-west-houston-evacuation-zone/2370185/

In terms of security, for groups of people that may want to reenter an evacuated area, first responders may need to implement a phased-reentry program including requisite credentials to govern the process.[2] First responders arriving at an evacuated area with restricted access must initially check-in at a designated Incident Command Post or staging area instead of directly responding to the affected area.

——————————— PRESERVING EVIDENCE ———————————

In the case of man-made disasters, public agents must preserve evidence. In addition to controlling access to a disaster area, emergency responders also have the legal authority to enter private property to resolve an emergency, including investigating the cause of the emergency. To remain on the property for investigation "officials need no warrant to remain for a reasonable time to investigate the cause of a blaze after it has been extinguished."[3] In order to determine a reasonable timeframe, one court has stated that the "[a]appropriate recognition must be given to the exigencies that confront officials serving under these conditions, as well as to individuals' reasonable expectations of privacy." The court added that, for the emergency responder, the appropriate expectation of privacy could "vary with the type of property, the amount of damage, prior and continued use of the premises, and in some cases, the owner's efforts to secure it against intruders."[4]. Therefore, we see that discernment and common sense are asked of emergency responders when giving content to the aforementioned notions.

As first responders also now receive tactical ballistic personal protective equipment (i.e., bullet-proof vests, helmets or trauma kits) at times, the roles of police, firefighters and emergency medical technicians may overlap during a disaster response. We can situate the latter, if first responders encounter illegal drug substances, paraphernalia or weapons while responding to a disaster, they do not have to confiscate the material themselves and act as police officers; they can call for the police to enter the property and take possession of the items.[5] As the Texas appellate court succinctly held in 2019 as a matter of the first impression that a police officer's entry into a defendant's apartment, after a firefighter who responded to a fire at the apartment observed contraband in plain view and asked the officer to lawfully secure the apartment.[6]

First responders may also need to protect evidence during a hazardous materials response caused by a man-made or natural calamity. Here the first responders, with or without the hazardous materials team, may enter the property to determine the risk to the public and to take samples to confirm the dangers associated with exposure to chemical or toxic substances. The same principles mentioned above also apply during hazardous material responses. Without the right to enter private property and, if necessary, collect samples that also effectively preserve evidence, first responders may themselves fall victim to toxic or chemical exposures.

A Court's Statement on Overlapping Roles

Police officers often fill many roles, including paramedic, social worker, and fire investigator . . . When those roles overlap the role of criminal investigator, it is not unreasonable to allow officers "to step into the shoes of" the firefighter to observe and to seize the contraband without first obtaining a warrant . . . Allowing this limited entry by an officer constitutes no greater intrusion upon the defendant's privacy interest than does a firefighter's entry . . . Under such circumstances, it would impose needless inconvenience and danger—to the firefighter, the officer, and the evidence—to require suspension of activity while a warrant is obtained . . . Firefighters' efforts are best devoted to fighting fire and sorting the aftermath, which are within their mission and core expertise. When, as here, the presence of firearms and contraband distracts from that mission, firefighters should be permitted to call upon police, whose expertise includes handling firearms and securing contraband.

Michigan v. Clifford, 464 U.S. 287; 104 S.Ct. 641 (1984)

Procedure dictates that oil spills in Texas require the responsible parties to immediately notify the Commissioner of the General Land Office (GLO) and undertake all reasonable actions to mitigate the pollution.[7] Local first responders and emergency managers responding to an oil spill will work under the GLO Commissioner, a state-designated on-scene coordinator and/or a federal on-scene coordinator.[8] Responders who voluntarily assist with the clean-up process according to the responsible person or the state or federal on-scene coordinators may enjoy qualified immunity for their response efforts.[9] The responsible party may refuse to comply with the GLO Commissioner's directions when they believe the GLO Commissioner's directions will unreasonably endanger public safety or natural resources or conflict with directions or orders of the federal on-scene coordinator.[10] For oil spills of 240 barrels or less, the Railroad Commission of Texas (RCT) is the on-scene coordinator.[11] For other types of petroleum spills or releases of hazardous waste and/or substances, the Texas Commission on Environment Quality (TCEQ) regulates the relationships between the state, the responsible party and the responders.[12] Based on the variety of designated on-scene coordinators as assigned by the appropriate state agency, information sharing between the emergency responders and the responsible party can be challenging. Adding to this complexity, the responsible party usually has more expertise and equipment to resolve an emergency incident. While responding to a chemical incident with little or no information about the on-scene chemicals is not uncommon, emergency responders do have some options to assist them with any lack of information sharing that may pose a risk to the responders and the community in general.

Engage in Planning and Practicing Spill Response

During the 2010 BP Oil Spill, first responders lacked the specialized equipment and requisite expertise to intervene and take control of the clean-up operations. As a result the national contingency plan was basically nullified, the public lost confidence in the Federal/BP response and the relationship with local/state officials deteriorated.[13] It was recommended to address this issue, that state and local leaders engage in the planning and practicing of spill response plans to prepare better to implement local emergency powers to aid in the response. This plan connects all three parties (responsible party, local leaders and first responders) and improves the partnerships for more effective responses.

Evacuation Area Protection

An increasing number of extreme weather events that deliver catastrophic flooding pose new risks to first responders when they manage evacuations zones. The 2017 investigation of the Arkema chemical incident during Hurricane Harvey revealed that multiple police officers and first responders were exposed to toxic chemicals while protecting the evacuation area 1.5 miles away.[14] The Chemical Safety Board (CSB) recommended the facility update its training procedures to assist with protecting first responders enforcing the evacuation perimeter as well as expanding protocols to include air monitoring equipment to provide protection when personnel are moved through an evacuation zone during a hazardous material release. When there is a chemical release due to natural disasters, joint efforts to identify appropriate road closures, evacuations routes, communication channels and personal protective equipment improve the shared knowledge of the chemicals on-hand and subsequent response activities. These recommendations are consistent with the BP Spill's recommendation in that both findings encourage more training and exercises between responders and facility operators.

Local Emergency Planning Committee (LEPC)

Information on chemical sites can also be shared through active participation in the community's LEPCs. A recent Texas guidebook for LEPCs showed an interesting paradox: the most successful LEPCs cited local government support as the most significant contributing factor, but it also stated that low participation (including local governments) was the greatest obstacle to success.[15] Local responders and emergency managers are a vital component in getting members' chemical information and establishing relationships with the chemical sector. To help this dilemma, emergency agencies could mandate participation in LEPC exercises through local ordinances or expanding departmental policies. For a thorough reference on this subject, the LEPC Executive Primer created by the Texas Division of Emergency Management (TDEM) is an excellent source.

Chemical Facility Anti-Terrorism Standards (CFATS)

1. Infrastructure Protection (I.P.) Gateway

In 2018 the US Government Accountability Office (GAO) identified the lack of information sharing for high-risk chemical facilities and other emergency personnel.[16] The Department of Homeland Security's (DHS) Chemical Facility Anti-Terrorism Standards (CFATS) program shares protected on-site chemicals through the IP Gateway, which may not be reported to either LEPCs or emergency responders. However, the GAO revealed that the IP Gateway was not widely used at the local level because local agencies did not know about the program and/or DHS did not sufficiently promote access to the IP Gateway. To improve chemical information for the emergency responders, DHS has improved its website to engage the IP Gateway program better and provides other essential actions to take to share information.[17]

2. Personnel Surety Program (PSP)

Private-sector emergency responders or public support agencies (i.e., power and communications) can obtain protected chemical information by requesting access to Chemical-terrorism Vulnerability Information (CVI). Because this information is highly protected, CVI may only be disclosed on a need-to-know basis except in exigent or emergency circumstances. However, in July 2019, DHS implemented the CFATS Personnel Surety Program (PSP) that can affect emergency responders who are not state and local officials but may need to gain unescorted access to restricted areas or critical assets during emergencies. This program can enhance the responder/responsible party relationship by developing pathways to work and train together while protecting chemical information.[18]

EMERGENCY CURFEWS

Federal and state laws delegate to local jurisdictions the authority to issue emergency curfews, and those jurisdictions usually issue curfews through an executive order that details the reasons for the curfew (i.e., clearing debris, preventing looting or repairing power outages.) Accordingly, the terms of the curfew order will list the scope, duration, area and penalties that police forces can enforce while still providing exceptions for first responders as needed.

COMMANDEERING PRIVATE PROPERTY

State law allows first responders to commandeer private property as required to use in coping with the disaster. Once the state exceeds its obligations and it needs the property/services for the disaster response, the governor can authorize the use or destruction of private property or services if the state provides compensation to the affected party. The compensation of compelled personal services, however, must have statutory authorization.[19]

HANDGUNS

In September 2019, the Texas Legislature expanded state handgun laws to declared disaster areas. A person is authorized to carry a handgun while evacuating from an area following a declaration of state disaster or a local state of disaster concerning that area, when: 1) reentering the area following the person's evacuation; 2) not more than 168 hours have elapsed since the governor declares a state of disaster or extends the time of the declaration; and 3) federal or state law does not otherwise prohibit the person from possessing a firearm.[20] Regarding shelters, Texas law authorizes possession of handguns at emergency shelter locations during state or local declared disasters when: 1) the owner, controller, operator of the premises or a person acting with the apparent authority of the same, authorizes the handgun carry; 2) the person carrying the handgun complies with any rules and regulations of the owner, controller or operator of the premises that govern the carrying of a handgun on the premises; and 3) the person is not prohibited by state or federal law from possessing a firearm.[21]

VIOLENCE AGAINST EMERGENCY MEDICAL SERVICES (EMS) RESPONDERS

For first responders, Texas law allows volunteer emergency services personnel to carry a handgun if they are engaged in providing emergency services and comply with the requirements for the state's concealed carry license laws.[22]

As a result of the rapid rise in violence against EMS responders, Emergency Medical Technicians (EMT) and Paramedics, the Center for Disease Control and Prevention (CDC) and the National Institute for Occupational Safety and Health (NIOSH) have determined the issue to be a workplace hazard.[23] Disaster stricken areas present high-risk and unstable working environments that expose EMS responders to further risk of violence.[24] Moreover, considering the limited police available during disaster response EMS workers are advised to not rely on the police to ensure their safety.[25] With growing violence directed at EMS and limited police forces, it has become frequently accepted for EMS responders to be trained in self-defense, like martial arts, to restrain aggressors when necessary.[26] However, like police officers, EMS departments have also used body armor and weapons like guns, tasers, mace and pepper spray.[27] In addition to these efforts other possible violence mitigation techniques include training in:

Scene size-up;	Entering a structure;
Weapons awareness;	Conflict management;
Weapons management;	Self-defense techniques;
Approaching the scene;	The legal issues surrounding self-defense;
Approaching the vehicle;	The use of force and cover and concealment techniques.

While the above list is not exhaustive, we offer it because the research on this topic shows that many of the existing violence reduction methods do not work well in the EMS industry.[28] Considering also that violence against EMS responders is a fairly recent risk offering violence mitigation techniques are consistent with the well-established general duty clause of the Texas Labor Code, Title 5. Workers' Compensation Act, Chapter 411.103, "Duty of Employer to Provide Safe Workplace," which states:

1. Provide and maintain employment and a place of employment that is reasonably safe and healthful for employees;

2. Install, maintain and use methods, processes, devices, and safeguards, including methods of sanitation and hygiene, that are reasonably necessary to protect the life, health, and safety of the employer's employees; and
3. Take all other actions reasonably necessary to make the employment and place of employment safe.

Texas Law on Self-Defense
Texas Penal Code § 9.31

It is beyond the scope of this framework to discuss the interesting details of self-defense rights, but Texas has a robust law on self-defense worth mentioning and covers topics like:

Whether the person reasonably believes that conduct was immediate necessary to protect one's self from another's use, or attempted use of unlawful force;
When is self-defense presumed to be "reasonable;" (i.e. during a sexual assault);
When is self-defense not justified (i.e. just venting);
When is self-defense forfeited (i.e. provoking as a pretext);
What degree of force is allowed (i.e. when the victim becomes the aggressor);
Whether there is there a duty to retreat; and
Can the victim pursue the attacker if they believe danger still exists?

MUTUAL AID AGREEMENTS

The increasing number of extreme weather events, hurricanes and chemical spill emergencies impose a lockstep rise in demand for emergency services. Local emergency responders typically meet these demands by using Mutual Aid Agreements and/or Memorandums of Understandings (MOU) to acquire additional personnel and equipment on an as-needed basis. From a legal perspective during disasters, however, these instruments share a common flaw: generally, when severe weather or large disasters (such as Hurricane Harvey) occur the widespread spike in demand will typically swamp local mutual aid response support resources and lessen their ability to fulfill their MOU commitments. In such situations, fire and police will have to draw upon regional and state plans to meet the demand through the Emergency Management Assistance Compact (EMAC). The Texas EMAC is managed by TDEM and offers a comprehensive guideline on how to reimburse individuals and jurisdictions for an EMAC deployment.[29]

Endnotes

[1] Tex. Gov. Code Ann. § 418.185.

[2] Tex. Gov't Code Ann. § 418.050.

[3] *Michigan v. Clifford*, 464 U.S. 287; 104 S.Ct. 641 (1984).

[4] *Id.*

[5] *Martin v. State of Texas*, 576 S.W.3d 818 (Tex. App. [Fort Worth] 2019).

[6] *Id.*

[7] Tex. Natural Resources Code Ann., § 40.101.

[8] Tex. Natural Resources Code Ann. § 40.102.

[9] Tex. Natural Resources Code Ann. § 40.104.

[10] Tex. Natural Resources Code Ann. § 40.107.

[11] Tex. Admin. Code Ann. Title 30m Part 1, § 327.1.

[12] Tex. Admin. Code Ann. Title 30, Part 1, § 327.2.

[13] Randle, Russell. "Spills of National Significance and State Nullification." *Ocean and Coastal Law Journal*, Volume 16, Number 2, Article 6. 2010.

[14] US Chemical Safety and Hazard Investigation Board. *Investigation Report: Organic Peroxide Decomposition, Release, and Fire at Arkema Crosby Following Hurricane Harvey Flooding*. May 2018. Report Number: 2017-08-I-TX.

[15] Trefz, B.A., and Bierling, D.H. *Local Emergency Planning Committee Executive Primer*. Produced by Texas A&M Transportation Institute for Texas Department of Public Safety, Division of Emergency Management. 2018.

[16] United States Government Accountability Office. *Critical Infrastructure Protection, DHS Should Take Actions to Measure Reduction in Chemical Facility Vulnerability and Share Information with First Responders*. GAO-18-538. August 2018.

[17] dhs.gov/publication/cfats-ipgateway.

[18] https://www.dhs.gov/cisa/cfats-personnel-surety-program.

[19] Tex. Gov't Code Ann. § 418.152.

[20] Tex. Penal Code § 46.15(k)(1).

[21] Tex. Penal Code § 46.15(l).

[22] Tex. Penal Code § 46.15(a)(10).

[23] Emergency Medical Services Workers: How Employees Can Prevent Injuries and Exposures. *Center for Disease Control and Prevention.* 2017. Available at https://www.cdc.gov/niosh/docs/2017-194/pdfs/2017-194.pdf.

[24] Murry, R.M., et al., *A Systemic Review of Workplace Violence Against Emergency Medical Services Responders.* A Journal of Environmental and Occupational Health Policy 0(0) 1-17. 2019.

[25] Mitigation of Occupational Violence to Firefighters and EMS Responders. *U.S. Fire Administration, FEMA.* June 2017.

[26] *Id* at p. 29.

[27] *Id* at p. 30.

[28] *Id.*

[29] Texas EMAC, https://tdem.texas.gov/emac.

PART 2

IDENTIFYING AUTHORITY

UNIFIED COMMAND

Texas' expansive definition of "disasters" includes both natural or man-made events, as well as oil spills, water or air contamination, energy emergencies and many others that stretch across the first responder spectrum.[1] Declaring a disaster activates the "state emergency management plan."[2] The state's emergency management plan follows the National Incident Management System (NIMS) in responding to disasters.[3] Under the NIMS approach, incidents that involve multiple agencies and/or jurisdictions with different legal, geographical and functional authorities mandate that they work together without affecting anyone agency's authority or responsibility.[4] Once engaged, the members of various state and local agencies will assemble according to NIMS and establish a Unified Command (UC) to coordinate the response activities. Members of the UC should have decision-making authority to respond and commit their respective resources to the joint enterprise.[5]

LEGAL AUTHORITY LANDSCAPE

Determining the lead agency in a UC structure can be difficult because every agency retains its own legal authority with its own decision-making discretion. For example, a spill of hazardous materials will initially prompt a local response from a local hazardous materials response team with the accompanying municipal environmental enforcement agencies.[6] The local agency may request assistance from the state for additional resources and agency coordination.[7] From here, TDEM may contact the state's lead agency on hazardous materials spills and air contamination, which is TCEQ.[8] If the substance involves oil that enters or threatens waterways, the lead agency changes to the General Land Office.[9] If the spill involves the exploration, development, production, including storage and pipeline transportation of oil, gas or geothermal resources, then the lead agency turns to the Railroad Commission of Texas.

Furthermore, if the spill affects the health of human beings, including radiation, this event points to the Texas Department of State Health Services.[10] Moreover, securing the site where the spill occurred may require the Texas Department of Public Safety.[11] Depending on the quantity and type of substance, as well as location, the hazard can prompt a federal response under separate national laws and other authorities.[12]

The shifting ability of disasters to require differing agencies and expertise challenges the responder's ability to identify who exactly is in charge of the event. The declaration of disaster can invoke the Incident Command System (ICS) as required by the NIMS directives and those commanders and agencies may further expand the structure of authority and increase the legal landscape determinations. Likewise, private organizations such as nursing homes and hospitals with high-life expectancy have their own hierarchy of command detailed in their emergency plans that should be designed to work with first responders. More will be discussed on this topic below.

Recommended Training for First Responders

To get firm footing on identifying who is in charge, first responders should be trained in the Incident Command System classes ICS-300 and ICS-400 and can be accessed through the Preparing Texas website (www.preparingtexas.gov). This training serves as the foundation to understanding the authority assignments made by the incident command system.

Table 1 below is an example of the primary responding agencies based on jurisdiction and reflects how the legal landscape changes during a disaster response as the support functions required also change.[13]

Table 1—Coordinating Agencies			
Jurisdictional Coordinators			
Emergency Support Function (ESF)	Federal Support Operations	State Support Operations	City (Houston) Support Operations
Transportation	Department of Transportation	Texas Department of Public Safety	Annex S
Communications	Department of Homeland Security (DHS)—National Communications System	Texas Department of Public Safety	Houston Emergency Center Annex B
Public Works and Engineering	Department of Defense US Army of Corps of Engineers	Texas Department of Transportation	Public Works and Engineering Annex L
Firefighting	US Forest Service	Texas A&M University Forest Service	Houston Fire Department Annex F
Emergency Management	DHS/Federal Emergency Management Agency (FEMA)	Texas Department of Emergency Management (TDEM)	Office of Emergency Management (OEM)
Mass Care, Human Services	DHS/FEMA	TDEM	Annex C
Logistics mgt, Resource Support	DHS/FEMA	TDEM	General Services Department Annex M
Public Health, Medical Services	Department of Health and Human Services	Texas Department of State Health Services	Houston Health Department Annex H

Table 1—Coordinating Agencies (Continued)			
Emergency Suport Function (ESF)	Federal Support Operations	State Support Operations	City (Houston) Support Operations
Search and Rescue	DHS/FEMA	Texas A&M University Texas Engineering Extension Service (TEEX)	Houston Fire Department Annex R
Oil and HAZMAT Response	Environmental Protective Agency (EPA)/US Coast Guard (USCG)	Texas Commission on Environmental Quality (TCEQ)	Houston Fire & Police Departments Annex Q
Agriculture and Natural Resources	Department of Agriculture	Texas Animal Commission Texas Dept. of Agriculture; Texas Dept. of State Health Services	None
Energy	Department of Energy	Public Utility Commission of Texas	None
Public Safety and Security	Department of Justice	TDEM	Houston Police Department Annex G
Long-Term Recovery	Replaced by the National Disaster Recovery Framework (NDRF)	TDEM	Annex J
External Affairs	DHS/FEMA	Texas Department of Public Safety	Annex I

After identifying the type of incident and determining the correct responding agency, the agencies that comprise the UC will have the responsibility to keep everyone informed of who is in charge and what functions are needed in the disaster response. With the assistance of the other ICS members (i.e., Incident Command, Liaison, Planning Section Chief), the UC should establish procedures to document command decisions, command staff positions and ensure updates from different response organizations into the ICS/UC enterprise.[14] These actions should keep everyone informed of who is in charge and the details regarding that position.

Tracking and updating personnel changes to the legal landscape of authorities is one of the top problems identified by members that have participated in a UC event. For emergency managers and first responders who are assigned to work in an Emergency Operations Center, the ambiguous and overlapping legal rules in determining "who is in charge" may inflame the types of disputes that inevitably arise in stressful events. To help with this problem, first responders operating in a UC enterprise may consider a few options to determine responsibility and accountability. Let us see them:

Legal Specialist. We know that the ICS allows for a legal specialist position in its planning section.[15] Likewise, an emergency plan's crosswalk will assign a legal office (i.e., the Attorney's General office) as the primary or supporting agency to respond to specific emergency functions.[16] However, this document suggests that the members of the UC themselves select an attorney trained in emergency management operations and alternative dispute resolution. Moreover, dedicating a seat at the Emergency Operations Center (EOC) for a trained and qualified attorney would specifically assist emergency managers and first responders in the field with real-time information funneled to the EOC through radio communications.

Example of an EOC Legal Counseling Position Task Book

Having fast, reliable and competent legal counseling was listed as a top priority by responders and managers that are assigned to an EOC, and in 2018 FEMA released its National Qualifications EOC Skillset Templates to help address this important need. The qualification skillset lists at least eight legal services an attorney is expected to be knowledgeable of and to advise EOC leadership and staff, like the UC enterprise, on relevant legal matters.

Compiling data from the TDEM, FEMA and the City of Houston, a sample EOC Legal Counseling Position Task Book was created to illustrate how local jurisdiction can use the information to train local attorneys who respond and operate in an emergency operations center. (Sample EOC Skillset: Legal Counseling).

https://www.fema.gov/media-library/assets/documents/170606

Operations Lawyer. Similar to legal experts that deploy with FEMA and military personnel, Operations Lawyers act much like a Texas All-Hazards Incident Management Teams (AHIMT) because they are NIMS/ICS compliant personnel trained in the roles of Operations "so that the Texas Department of Emergency Management (TDEM) can have the same counterparts as local and federal partners."[17] To qualify for membership on an AHIMT the individual must have completed a task book detailing the training and experience received.[18]

Research shows that through training with first responders in table-top exercises, participating in disaster exercises and attending emergency services continuing education courses dramatically increases the effectiveness of the joint-professional (attorney-first responder) relationship. By way of example, FEMA recognizes this significant relationship and agrees that having lawyers trained in EOC operations and possessing the intellectual readiness needed in the response phase of a disaster played a crucial role in enabling the successful delivery of legal advice.[19]

Endnotes

[1] Tex. Gov. Code § 418.004(1).

[2] Tex. Gov. Code § 418.015(1).

[3] State of Texas Emergency Management Plan. Basic Plan February 2019.

[4] National Incident Command System. US Department of Homeland Security, December 2008, https://www.fema.gov/pdf/emergency/nims/NIMS_core.pdf.

[5] Unified Command: Technical Assistance Document. The National Response Team.

[6] City of Houston Ordinances, Section 34-61, Hazardous materials response team service.

[7] Texas Government Code § 418.042(a)(11).

[8] Texas Water Code § 26.261; Texas Health & Safety Code § 382.001.

[9] Texas Natural Resources Code § 40.001.

[10] Texas Health & Safety Code § 401.0005.

[11] Texas Government Code § 418.041.

[12] Civins, Jeff, and Scanlon, Michael. *Environmental Issues Associated with Disaster Planning and Response. Key Environmental Issues in Region.* June 11, 2019, Atlanta, Georgia. American Bar Association, Section on Environmental, Energy, and Resources.

[13] Disaster Operations Legal Reference, ver. 2.0, *FEMA*, June 1, 2013; State of Texas Emergency Management Plan. February 2019. *TDEM*; City of Houston Emergency Management Plan, *COHOEM*, 2016.

[14] Unified Command Technical Assistance Document. U.S. National Response Team, § 1.1.3.

[15] *Supra*, note 4.

[16] *Supra*, note 3.

[17] Texas Emergency Management Online. 2012 Volume 59, Number 6. Http://dps.texas.gov/dem/temoArchives/2012/Vol59No06/index.html.

[18] http://ticc.tamu.edu/response/ahimt.htm.

[19] Advice in Crisis: Towards Best Practices for Providing Legal Advice under Disaster Conditions. Appendix A, *Disaster Operations Legal Reference*. FEMA. Version 2.0 June 1, 2013.

PART 3

RESPONSIBILITY, ACCOUNTABILITY & LIABILITY

Determining personal liability requires a complex analysis that weaves through different levels of both federal, state and local laws. Limiting our analysis to Texas' laws, we generally know lawsuits brought against a government employee are immediately dismissed.[1] However, if the lawsuit alleges the employee's misconduct fell within their scope of employment, the court will deem the suit against the employee's official capacity and will dismiss the claim against the employee and, possibly, amend the suit to include the correct government body.[2] While this protection sets a high bar, it may be helpful nonetheless to review where Texas has waived immunity to get a deeper understanding of the potential liability that might arise from the employee's official capacity. The liability issue most relevant to disaster response includes issues of statutory liability, gross negligence, intentional conduct and state-created dangers. These causes of action must always interact with the first responder's right to official immunity, which in turn rests on the responder's "scope of employment" and discretionary duties.

When A Government Agency Is Not Liable

The government is not liable for performing acts that are: 1) not required by law; or 2) on failure to make a decision on the performance or nonperformance of an act, if the law leaves the performance of the act to the discretion of the government agency.

Tex. Civ. Prac. & Rem. Code Ann. § 101.056

—————— STATE EMERGENCY MANAGEMENT LAWS ——————

The state emergency management laws limit liability depending on the function performed. Statutory immunity exists when a state employee performs an activity related to sheltering or housing in connection with an evacuation of an area stricken or threatened by a disaster.[3] Also, a public servant carrying out a mandatory evacuation order gains immunity for any act or omission within the course and scope of the person's authority under the evacuation order.[4] Regarding state, local or interjurisdictional emergency management plans, Texas allows local jurisdictions to implement fines or jail confinement in their own emergency response plans if a person fails to comply with a rule, order or ordinance adopted under the plan.[5] One must review the respective plans to determine if this clause was included as a basis of personal liability.

18

Texas homeland security laws limit civil liability if a person performs a defined homeland security activity under specific procedures or circumstances and acts within the person's authority.[6] However, those laws deny immunity from civil liability if the person acts willfully or wantonly negligent or acts with conscious indifference or reckless disregard for the safety of others the homeland security laws intend to protect.[7] As recently as 2019, the Texas legislature updated the state's homeland security law to classify 911 operators as first responders, affecting immunity protections for persons giving emergency care.[8]

MUNICIPAL ORDINANCES

For municipalities, emergency response liability insulates them from damages that arise from their government functions, such as police and fire protection, health services and emergency ambulance operations if they exercise them in the interest of the general public.[9] In addition to the traditional fire and police protection, agency liability also includes emergency management and homeland security organizations which relate to the governor's statewide homeland security strategy and responds to Texas Department of Emergency Management (TDEM).[10]

The statute preserves explicitly municipal immunity for other related duties such as responding or reacting to an emergency event (or failing to provide such services); or in selecting the method used to provide police or fire protection.[11] However, municipal ordinances can carve out waivers of immunity for employees in specific events such as operating motor vehicles or motorized equipment (i.e., drones), or employees who, while acting within the scope of employment, commit wrongful acts and omissions, or negligently fail to meet other liability standards.[12] Likewise, municipal liability may attach when a three-part test is satisfied:

1) a policymaker is involved;
2) an existing official policy is in place; and
3) a violation of constitutional rights whose "moving force" is the policy or custom.[13]

Table 2 "Disaster Response Laws Comparison" provides a side-by-side comparison of these three types of laws.

Table 2: Disaster Response Laws Comparison

Emergency Management TGC 418.006	Homeland Security TGC 421.061	Government Immunity TCRP 101
Officer or employee of a state or local agency	Officer or employee of a state or local agency or volunteer(421.001(1) "agency"means any government entity)	A government unit is liable for 101.001(3) A government unit is: A. State agencies, departments, bureaus, etc.; B. Cities, counties, districts, etc.; C. Emergency management organization (formed and operated under 421.002 and responsive to TDEM under 418.112)
Performing an activity related to sheltering or housing activity related to sheltering or housing	Performing a "homeland security activity."(421.001(3) "Homeland security activity" means any activity related to the prevention or discovery of, response to, or recovery from: 1. A terrorist attack; 2. A natural or man-made disaster; 3. A hostile military or paramilitary action; 4. An extraordinary law enforcement emergency; 5. Or a fire or medical emergency that requires resources beyond the capabilities of a local jurisdiction	• Property damage, personal injury and death; • Proximately caused by wrongful act, omission or negligence of an employee; • Acting within the scope of employment, if a. Operating or using a vehicle or motor-driven equipment; and b. The employee would be personally liable according to Texas law. (OR)

Table 2: Disaster Response Laws Comparison (continued)

Emergency Management TGC 418.006	Homeland Security TGC 421.061	Government Immunity TCRP 101
Does the disaster include the occurrence or imminent threat of: 1. Widespread or severe damage; 2. Injury or loss of life or property resulting from any natural or man-made cause; 3. Fire; 4. Flood; 5. Earthquake; 6. Wind; 7. Storm; 8. Wave action; 9. Oil spill or other water contamination; 10. Volcanic activity; 11. Epidemic; 12. Air contamination; 13. Blight; 14. Drought; 15. Infestation; 16. Explosion; 17. Riot; 18. Hostile military or paramilitary action; 19. Extreme heat; 20. Other public calamity requiring emergency action or energy emergency.	Performing at the request or under the direction of an officer or employee of a state or local agency	(2) • Personal injury and death; • Caused by a condition or use of tangible personal or real property; • If the government unit would were it a private person; • Be liable according to Texas law. Exceptions & Exclusions § 101.055 This chapter does not apply to a claim arising from:

Officer or employee of a state or political subdivision (418.004(6) "political subdivision" means a county or incorporated city)	Performing the homeland security activity under procedures prescribed or circumstances described in the governor's homeland security strategy	(1)
		• From action of an employee responding to an emergency call; or
		• Reacting to emergencies;
		• In compliance with laws applicable to emergency action; or
		• If no law exists, then action not taken with:
		  a. Conscious indifference; or
		  b. Reckless disregard for the safety of others
		(OR)

Table 2: Disaster Response Laws Comparison (continued)

Emergency Management TGC 418.006	Homeland Security TGC 421.061	Government Immunity TCRP 101
Issued or is working to carry out a mandatory evacuation Acting within the course and scope of the person's authority under the order	Acting within the course and scope of the person's authority (if a volunteer, then within the course and scope of the request or direction of the officer or employee of the state or local agency) Exception: potential liability for damages resulting from performing a homeland security activity, if under the circumstances, was: 1. Willfully or wanton negligence; or 2. With conscious indifference; or Reckless disregard for the safety of persons	(2) • From the failure to provide; or • The method of providing; • Police and fire protection Liability of Municipality § 101.0215 For damages arising from its government function (non-exhaustive list including police and fire protection, health and emergency ambulance services)

INTENTIONAL CONDUCT

As discussed above, Texas law imposes liability for a person's conduct, depending, in part, on the intention underlying the act itself. As a result, it is critical to understand how Texas law defines the different standards of conduct.

Intentional Acts. The Texas penal code defines this element as when a person "acts intentionally, or with intent, concerning the nature of his conduct or to a result of his conduct when it is his conscious objective or desire to engage in the conduct of cause the result."[14]

Knowingly Acts. In close relation, intention can be synonymous with knowledge and the penal code guides this definition as to when a person acts "knowingly" or with knowledge, concerning a result of his conduct when he is aware that his conduct is reasonably certain to cause the result.[15]

Reckless Acts. A person acts "recklessly" or is reckless with respect to circumstances surrounding his conduct or the result of his conduct when he is aware of but consciously disregards a substantial and unjustifiable risk that the circumstances exist or the result will occur. The risk must be of such a nature and degree that its disregard constitutes a gross deviation from the standard of care that an ordinary person would exercise under all the circumstances as viewed from the actor's standpoint.[16]

When the responder's conduct is not intentional or reckless, it still can be negligent if a person failed to take proper care in performing some action. Public responders typically face liability only if they act with gross negligence and any action that fails a gross negligent standard will, by definition, also constitute standard negligence.

Standard Negligence. This cause of action must satisfy three elements: 1) the existence of a legal duty; 2) a breach of that duty; and 3) damages that were caused by the breach of duty.[17] These three elements cannot be satisfied by mere conjecture, guess or speculation. In particular, the damages element that includes the proximate cause consist of two additional factors: 1) cause-in-fact and 2) foreseeability.[18]

Cause-in-fact is established when the act or omission was a substantial factor in bringing about the injuries, and without it, the harm would not have occurred.[19]

Foreseeability exists when the actor, as a person of ordinary intelligence, should have anticipated the dangers his negligence act creates for others.[20]

Gross Negligence. For government actors such as public first responders, liability requires a higher standard of gross negligence. This standard requires two other elements in addition to standard negligence, which are:

1) an act or omission which when viewed objectively from the standpoint of the actor at the time of its occurrence involves an extreme degree of risk, considering the probability and magnitude of the potential harm to others; and
2) of which the actor has actual, subjective awareness of the risk involved, but nevertheless proceeds with conscious indifference to the rights, safety or welfare of others.[21]

A review of relevant liability laws will use a variety of similar terms to convey the action of "gross negligence," and the courts have equated "gross negligence" with willful negligence, conscious indifference to the welfare of others and reckless disregard for the rights of others;[22] including willful negligence, or done with conscious indifference or reckless disregard for the safety of others.[23] For example, under the Texas homeland, security law immunity is waived for activities done with "willful for wanton negligence or with conscious indifference." Likewise, under the governmental immunity law, liability may attach for acts of reckless disregard for the safety of others. See Table 2 for the full text of these two statutes[24].

Further defining terms of liability, one court held that to establish "deliberate indifference," the environment created by the state actors must be dangerous; they must know it is dangerous, and they must have used their authority to create an opportunity that would not otherwise have existed for the third party's crime to occur.[25] More on this subject follows in the next pages.

SPECIAL RELATIONSHIP I: FAILURE TO ACT

Texas law does not impose any general duty for first responders to protect citizens from the invasion of private actors. However, government liability may attach in two distinct occasions when assistance is called for: 1) when there is a "special relationship" between the public responder and the person requesting assistance, and 2) when the state exposes a person to a danger of its own making (i.e., state-created danger).[26] To date, a "special relationship" only exists if the person is involuntarily confined against their will through affirmative exercise of police power.[27] Without this type of special relationship, the state has no duty to protect, nor liability from, failing to protect persons at the hands of private actors.[28]

Consistent with the absence of a duty to protect the general public at large from other private actors, when conditions become too dangerous for first responders like during a hurricane, restricting or denying emergency service operations for a limited time is acceptable to protect the first responders. The length of the acceptable time to halt response operations will depend on departmental directions and policies. For example, sustained winds of 39 mph generally are acceptable thresholds for the "no-go" determination for first responders.[29]

SPECIAL RELATIONSHIP II: STATE-CREATED DANGER

The federal courts have not adopted the "state-created danger" theory of liability,[30] but Texas state courts have recognized this argument. Liability under this doctrine "lies in the state actor's culpable knowledge and conduct in affirmatively placing an individual in a position of danger, effectively stripping a person of her ability to defend herself or cutting off potential sources of private aid."[31] The two basic requirements of a state-created danger theory are: 1) a plaintiff must show that the state actors increased the danger to the plaintiff, and 2) that the state actors acted with deliberate indifference.[32] For the element of deliberate indifference, the act must involve a dangerous environment created by the state actors; they must know it is dangerous and they must have used their authority to create an opportunity that would not otherwise have existed for the third party's crime to occur.[33]

In a related situation, government agencies may face liability if they fail to train their first responders to recognize when a victim in their custody requires medical aid.[34] For instance, police officers who use lethal force but fail to provide medical aid, or fail to call for medical assistance, can create both a special relationship and requisite knowledge for medical aid sufficient to impose potential liability.

No State-Created Danger If Provide Alternative Rescue Efforts

Where county sheriffs prevented rescue efforts attempted by volunteer firefighters, which could have limited the victim's injuries related to the spilled chlorine gas from a train derailment, but did manage a delayed rescue by career firefighters, the court stated that there was no state-created danger because: 1) they did not create the immediate danger of the leaking gas, including the fact that the delayed rescue did not show the sheriffs increased a person's vulnerability by interference with protective services which otherwise would be available; and 2) the sheriffs did not fail to take action to alleviate the danger, rather they substituted the rescue efforts with career firefighters instead of volunteer firefighters.

Hale v. Bexar County, Tex., 342 Fed. Appx. 921 (2009)

POLICE AND FIREFIGHTER EMPLOYMENT DISCIPLINE: TEXAS CIVIL SERVICE PROTECTION, CHAPTER 143

If a police officer or firefighter operates in a jurisdiction that has adopted relevant provisions of the Texas Civil Service statute, a police officer or firefighter may face disciplinary action, including indefinite suspension for behaviors that display incompetence, neglect of duty and "shirking duty or cowardice at fires."[35]

New Texas First Responders: 911 Dispatchers

In 2019 various statutes changed the definition of "first responders" to include 911 dispatchers. The changes will not only affect statues like the health and safety code, labor code and immunity protection laws, but also will give dispatchers recognition with fire, police and emergency medical services.

STATE OFFICIAL IMMUNITY

The Texas Supreme Court recognizes official immunity as an affirmative defense for law enforcement and emergency response personnel, entitling them to official immunity from suits arising from the performance of their: 1) discretionary duties done in 2) good faith; as long as they are 3) acting within the scope of their authority.[36]

Discretionary duties in this context refer to any action taken that involves personal deliberation, decision and judgment.[37] In contrast, ***ministerial acts*** leave nothing to the exercise of discretion or judgment and if a public official must obey an order with no choice in complying, then the act is ministerial.[38]

Example of Discretionary Duty: Emergency Call Operator

Although the emergency operator's job appeared to be ministerial and only transcribe information from callers, considering the urgency involved in emergency situations, the emergency operator had to use discretion when interpreting and then classifying and transcribing 911 calls, and was therefore granted immunity from liability for misclassifying the call response level.

Beltran v. City of El Paso, 367 F.3d 299 (5th Cir. 2004)

Because some of these laws require that actions fall within the "scope of employment" or "scope of authority" before they can qualify for immunity, it is helpful to have a definition of those concepts and how Texas laws apply them when considering government immunity.

Scope of Employment means the "performance for a government unit of the duties of an employee's office or employment and includes being in or about the performance of a task lawfully assigned to an employee by the competent authority."[39]

Other statutes may use the term **"Scope of Authority."** At least one Texas court has equated the two terms and confirmed that the focus is not on the employee's authority to commit an act, but rather whether the employee discharged duties normally assigned to them.[40]

Example of "Outside" the Scope of Employment

In general, when conduct has nothing to do with an employee's duties, it can be alleged that the acts are outside the scope of employment or authority. For example, when an on-duty police officer kisses a fellow officer without consent; or when a judge's secretary causes a fatal car accident while driving her personal car to a doctor's appointment, are examples of actions not related to the employee's normal job duties.

Kelemen v. Elliot, 260 S.W.3d 518 (Tex. App.—Houston [1st Dist.] 2008) and
Terrell ex re. Estate of Terrell v. Sisk, 111 S.W.3d 274 (Tex. App.—Texarkana, 2003)

Government immunity does not protect every act by a government employee exercising judgment. Public officials still may act without legal authority, and thus be "ultra vires," if the official exceeds the bounds of her granted authority or if her acts conflict with the law itself.[41] An *ultra vires* claim based on actions taken "without legal authority" has two fundamental components: (1) authority giving the official some (but not absolute) discretion to act; and (2) engaging in conduct outside of that authority.[42]

"Sovereign immunity" bars suits complaining of an exercise of *absolute* discretion. However, it allows actions contending that an officer's exercise of judgment, or *limited* discretion, unrelated to (or in conflict with) the limits set out by the underlying law that authorizes the official to act."[43] A government official acts *"beyond his granted discretion"* if he "exercises judgment or limited discretion 'without reference to or in conflict with the constraints of the law authorizing the official to act,' because 'a public officer has no discretion or authority to misinterpret the law.'"[44]

To fall within this *ultra vires* exception, a suit must not complain of a government officer's exercise of discretion. It instead must allege, and ultimately prove, that the officer acted without legal authority or failed to perform a purely ministerial act.[45] "Ministerial acts," on the other hand, are those "where the law prescribes and defines the duties to be performed with such precision and certainty as to leave nothing to the exercise of discretion or judgment."[46]

However, it is not an *ultra vires* act for government officials to make an erroneous decision while staying within their authority.[47]

Under federal law, a government entity can incur liability only if its official policy or custom deprives a person of a federally protected right.[48] Moreover, a successful claimant must show that the governmental entity, through its deliberate conduct, was the moving force causing the injury. The claimant must establish a direct causal link between the entity's action and the deprivation of the federally protected right.[49]

Government officials who perform discretionary functions enjoy qualified federal immunity from liability for civil damages if their conduct does not violate clearly established statutory, constitutional rights that a reasonable person would know.[50] A right is "clearly established" when it is apparent to the public official that his or her actions are unlawful in light of pre-existing law, and not merely improper or questionable.[51] The notion of "reasonable person" in this sense is based on whether other public officers (first responders) could agree if the challenged conduct is legal or not.[52]

Example of Equal Protection Violation

While there is no special relationship formed during common responses to emergencies, the equal protection clause may impose one in certain situations. For instance, once emergency responders "make an effort to communicate with and extract information from a person, the public entity has a duty, under the American with Disabilities Act, to ensure that a disabled person is 'afforded . . . an equal opportunity to benefit from the services provided by the [city] to those who do not suffer from a hearing-impairment.'"

Salinas v. City of New Braunfels, 557 F.Supp.2d 777
(W.D. Tex. Div—San Antonio 2008); 36 NDLR P 191

Endnotes

[1] Tex. Civ. Prac. & Rem. Code Ann. § 101.106(e).

[2] Tex. Civ. Prac. & Rem. Code Ann. § 101.106(f).

[3] Tex. Gov't Code § 418.006.

[4] Tex. Gov't Code § 418.185.

[5] Tex. Gov't Code § 418.173.

[6] Tex. Gov't Code § 421.061(a).

[7] Tex. Gov't Code § 421.061(b).

[8] HB1090, 86th Legislative Session.

[9] Tex. Civ. Prac. & Code Ann. § 101.0215.

[10] Tex. Civ. Prac. & Rem. Code Ann. § 101.001.

[11] Tex. Civ. Prac. & Rem. Code Ann. § 101.055.

[12] Tex. Civ. Prac. & Rem. Code Ann. § 101.021.

[13] *Piotrowski v. City of Houston*, 237 F.3d 567 (5th Cir., 2001).

[14] Tex. Penal Code § 6.03(a).

[15] Tex. Penal Code § 6.03(b).

[16] Tex. Penal Code § 6.03(c).

[17] *IHS Cedars Treatment Center of DeSoto, Texas, Inc., v. Mason*, 47 Tex. Sup. Ct. J. 666, 143 S.W.3d 764, (Tex., 2004).

[18] *D. Houston v. Love*, 45 Tex. Sup. Ct. J. 943; 92 S.W.3d 450 (2002).

[19] *Bustamante* at note 22.

[20] *D. Houston supra* at note 24.

[21] Tex. Civ. Prac. & Rem. Code Ann. § 41.001(11).

[22] *Burk Royalty Co. v. Walls*, 616 S.W.2d 911, (Tex. 1981).

[23] *Chrisman v. Brown*, 246 S.W.3d 102 (Tex.App.-Houston [14th Dist.] 2007, no pet.).

[24] See page 44.

[25] *Piotrowski supra* at note 57.

[26] *DeShaney v. Winnebago County*, 109 S,Ct. 998 (1989); 489 U.S. 189; 103 L.Ed.2d 249.

[27] *Walton v. Alexander*, 44 F.3d 1297 (5th Cir. 1995).

[28] *Id.*

[29] Special Report: Fire Department Preparedness for Extreme Weather Emergencies and Natural Disasters. US Fire Administration/Technical Report Series. USFA-TR-162/April 2008. Retrieved from https://www.usfa.fema.gov/downloads/pdf/publications/tr_162.pdf.

[30] *Randolph v. Cervantes*, 130 F.3d 737 (5th Cir. 1997).

[31] *Johnson v. Dallas Indep. Sch. Dist.* 38 F.3d 198 (5th Cir. 1994).

[32] *Piotrowski, supra* at note 57.

[33] *Id.*

[34] *City of Canton, Ohio v. Harris*, 489 U.S. 378 (1989).

[35] Tex. Loc. Gov't Code Ann., § 143.051.

[36] *Ballantyne v. Champion Builders, Inc.*, 47 Tex. Sup. Ct. J. 852 (2004); 144 S.W.3d 417.

[37] *Wyse v. Department of Public Safety*, 733 S.W.2d 224 (Tex. App.-Waco, 1986).

[38] *Ballantyne, supra* note 81.

[39] Tex. Civ. Prac. & Rem. Code Ann. § 101.005(5).

[40] *Wilkerson v. University of North Texas By and Through Board of Regents*, 878 F.3d 147 (5th Cir. 2017).

[41] *Houston Belt & Terminal Railway Co., v. City of Houston*, 59 Tex. Sup. Ct. J. 512 (2016); 487 S.W.3d 154.

[42] *Id.* at 158.

[43] *Id.* at 163.

[44] *Chambers–Liberty Counties Navigation Dist.*, 2019 WL 2063575.

[45] *City of El Paso v. Heinrich*, 52 Tex. Sup. Ct. J. 689 (2009); 284 S.W.3d 366.

[46] *Sw. Bell Tel., L.P. v. Emmett*, 58 Tex. Sup. Ct. J. 567 (2015); 459 S.W.3d 578.

[47] *Hall v. McRaven*, Tex. Sup. Ct. J. 315 (2017); 508 S.W.3d 232.

[48] *Graham v. Dallas Area Rapid Transport*, 288 F.Supp.3d 711 (N.D. Tex. Div.—Dallas 2017).

[49] *Bryan County v. Brown*, 520 U.S. 404, 117 S.Ct. 1382 (1997); 137 L.Ed.2d 626.

[50] *Mullenix v. Luna*, 136 S.Ct. 305 (2015); 193 L.Ed.2d 255; 84 USLW 3254; citing *Pearson v. Callahan*, 555 U.S. 223, 129 S.Ct. 808 (2009).

[51] *Graham, supra* at note 94.

[52] *Id.*

APPENDIX A
FIELD GUIDEBOOK FLOWCHARTS

COMPENSATION FOR COMMANDEERING PROPERTY AND SERVICES

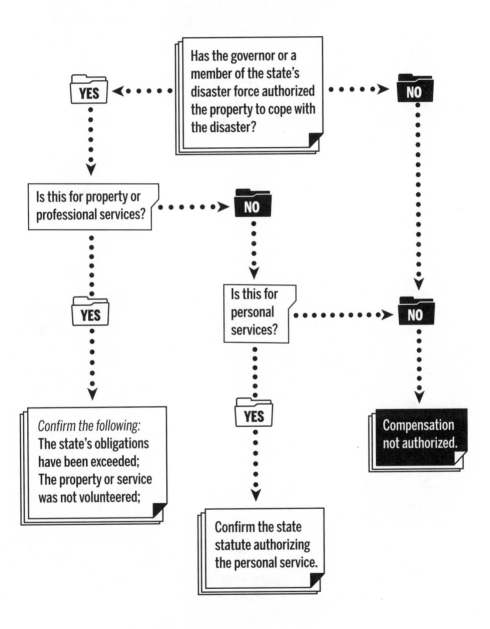

STATE-CREATED DANGER

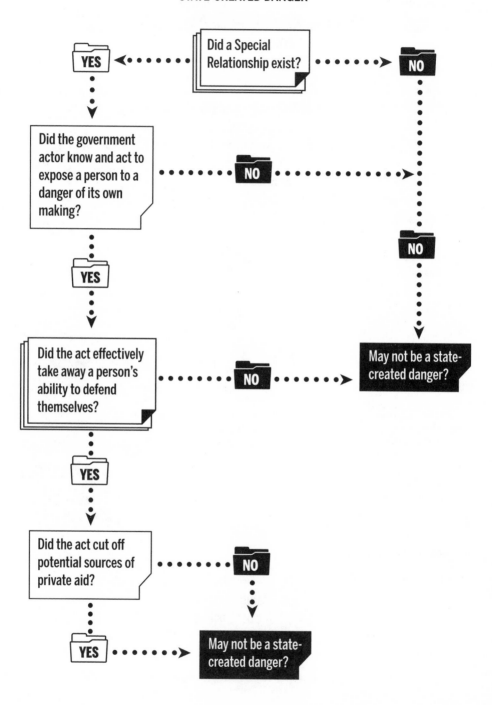

GROSS NEGLIGENCE

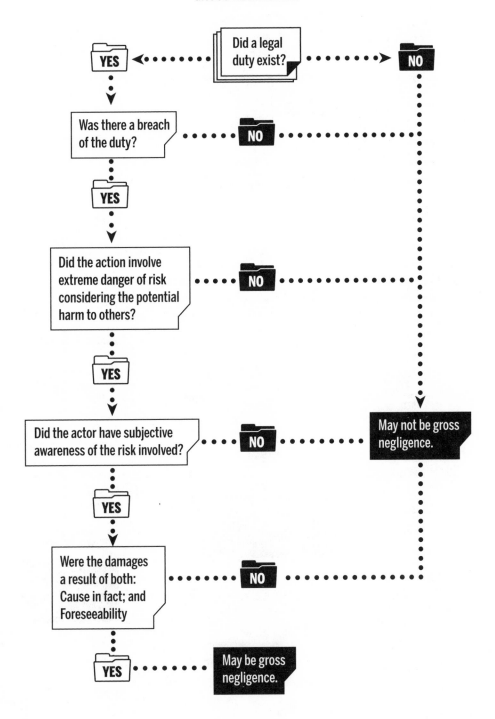

STATE OFFICIAL IMMUNITY

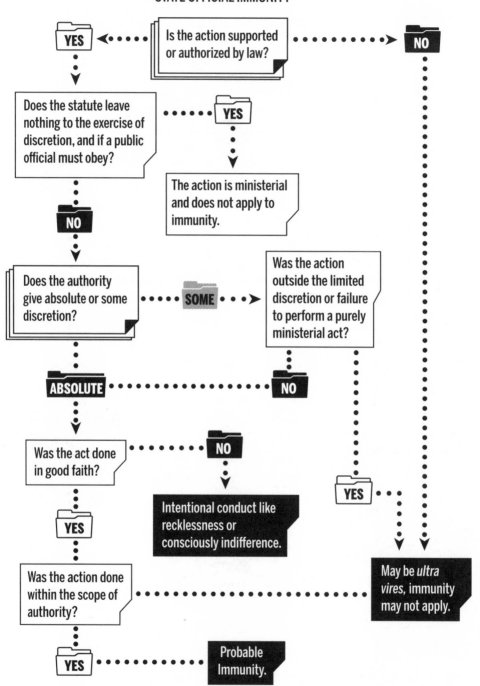

GOVERNMENTAL IMMUNITY

Does the issue concern a Federal or Texas constitutional right or statute?

Federal

Texas

Confirm the following:
The federal constitutional right or statue was clearly established; and
A reasonable person would have known about the federal constitutional or statutory right.

Confirm the following:
The action was required by state law; The act was a discretionary duty; The act was done in good faith; and The act was within the scope of authority.

Are all the elements satisfied?

NO

Probably no immunity.

May see State Official Immunity flowchart.

YES

Probable Immunity.

APPENDIX B

SAMPLE EOC SKILLSET: LEGAL COUNSELING

Tasks	Code	Evaluation Record #	Evaluator Initials and Date
1. At the local, state, trial, territorial and federal levels, demonstrate knowledge of:	E, F, I, J		

LOCAL
- City of Houston, City Charter, as amended
- City of Houston, Code of Ordinances,
- City of Houston, Code of Ordinances, Chapter 13, Emergency Management
- City of Houston, Code of Ordinances, Chapter 2, Article II, Division 1 Generally, Section 2-28
- City of Houston, Mayor Executive Order 1-25, Exerciser of Mayor's Emergency Authority during a Local State of Disaster
- City of Houston, Mayor Executive Order 1-49, Adopting the National Incident Management System
- City of Houston, Administrative Policy 4.2, Internal Disaster Preparation & Recovery

STATE
- Constitution of the State of Texas
- Texas Education Code, Chapter 88, §§ 88.112—88.116
- South Central Interstate Forest Fire Protection Compact
- Texas Government Code:
  o Chapter 411 Texas Department of Public Safety
  o Chapter 418 Emergency Management
  o Chapter 421 Homeland Security
  o Chapter 433 State of Emergency
  o Chapter 791 Interlocal Cooperative Contracts
  o Texas Health and Safety Code, Title 9, Subtitle B, Chapter 778 Emergency Management Assistance Compact
- Texas Local Government Code
  o Title 6, Chapter 616 Emergency Interim Public Office Succession Act
  o Title 12, Chapter 391 Regional Planning Commissions

Tasks	Code	Evaluation Record #	Evaluator Initials and Date

• Texas Administrative Code, Title 37, Part 1, Chapter 7, Division of Emergency Management
• Texas Governor Executive Orders
  o GA 05—Relating to Emergency Management of Natural and Human-Caused Events, Emergencies, and Disasters (2018)
  o R.P. 1—Relating to Emergency Management (2001)
  o PR 8—Relating to the Governor's Task Force on Homeland Security (2001)
  o R.P. 16—Relating to the Creation of the Statewide Texas Amber Alert Network (2002)
  o R.P. 40—Relating to the Designation of the National Incident Management System as the Incident Management System for the State of Texas (2005)
  o R.P. 48—Relating to the Expedition Restoration of Electrical Services in Areas Damaged by Hurricane Rita (2005)
  o R.P. 59—Relating to the Renewal of Disaster Recovery Issues due to the Effects of Hurricanes Katrina and Rita (2005)
  o R.P. 68—Relating to the Creation of Blue Alert Program (2008)
  o R.P. 69—Relating to the Creation of the Governor's Commission for Disaster Recovery and Renewal (2008)
  o Texas Homeland Security Strategic Plan 2015-2020
  o State of Texas Emergency Management Plan 2019
 	
FEDERAL
• Robert T. Stafford Disaster Relief and Emergency Assistance Act, Public Law 93-288m as amended
• 42 U.S. Code § 5170 (2013, January 29) Procedure for Declaration
• Post-Katrina Emergency Management Reform Act (PKEMRA), 2006			

Tasks	Code	Evaluation Record #	Evaluator Initials and Date

• National Response Framework (NRF), January 2008
• Housing and Economic Recovery Act of 2008
• FEMA REP Manual/NUREG 0654, April 2012
• The National Security Strategy, May 2010
• Emergency Management and Assistance, Code of Federal Regulations (CFR) 44
• Price-Anderson Amendments Act of 1988, Public Law 100-408, as amended
• Emergency Management Assistance Compact, Public Law 104-321
• National Incident Management Systems (NIMS), December 2008
• Homeland Security Presidential Directives:
  o HSPD 3: Homeland Security Advisory System, March 2002
  o HSPD 5: Management of Domestic Incidents. February 2003
  o HSPD 7: Critical Infrastructure Identification, Prioritization, and Protection, December 2003
  o HSPD 8: National Preparedness, March 2011
• Americans with Disabilities Act (ADA) of 1990
• ADA Guide for Local Governments, US Department of Justice, July 2005
• Sandy Recovery Improvement Act (SIRA) of 2013
• Disaster Relief Appropriations Act of 2013
• Executive Order 13347, Federal Register, Individual with Disabilities in Emergency Preparedness
• Guidance on Planning for Integration of Functional Needs Support Services (FNSS) in General Population Shelters, November 2010
• Developing and Maintaining Emergency Operations Plans: Comprehensive Preparedness Guide (CPG) 101: Version 2.0 November 2010			

Tasks	Code	Evaluation Record #	Evaluator Initials and Date
2. At the local, state, tribal, territorial, and federal levels, demonstrate knowledge of procurement laws and procedures. • Texas Local Government Code, Chapter 252 Purchasing & Contracting Authority of Municipalities • Texas Government Code, Chapter 2254 Professional & Consulting Services • Texas Local Government Code, Chapter 271 Purchasing & Contracting Authority of Municipalities, Counties & Other Certain Local Governments • City of Houston, Code of Ordinances, Chapter 15, Article III Contracts, Procurement • City of Houston, Mayor's Executive Order 1-14, Procurement and Payment Policies • City of Houston, Mayor's Executive Order 1-52, Procurement Governance Board • City of Houston, Administrative Policy 5-7, Procurement Standards • City of Houston, Administrative Policy 5-8, Informal Procurement • City of Houston, Administrative Policy, 5-11, Exceptions to Competitive Procurements • FEMA Public Assistance Program and Policy Guide, FP 104-009-2 / April 2018	E, F, I, J		
3. Demonstrate knowledge of: a. Mutual Aid Agreements (MAA) City of Houston, Basic Emergency Plan, Chapter 10, Section 10.2.2, Tab 4—List of Agreements and Contracts b. Memorandum of Understanding (MOU) MOU—A document that describes very broad concepts of mutual understanding, goals and plans shared by the parties. c. Memorandum of Agreement (MOA) MOA—A document describing in detail the specific responsibilities and actions to be taken by each of the parties so that their mutual goals may be accomplished. A MOA may also indicate the goals of the parties, to help explain their actions and responsibilities.			

Tasks	Code	Evaluation Record #	Evaluator Initials and Date
4. Brief or inform EOC personnel about legal advice available to guide EOC activities. Performance Criteria for legal advice (SALT) produced by a legal officer. • Solution-Oriented—Focus on legally viable solutions and outcomes, and create solutions to legal problems; help to resolve conflicts, and eliminate barriers consistent with the agency mission. • Articulate—state legal positions and explanations in an organized, well-reasoned and persuasive manner; limit the use of "legalese." • Legally Sufficient—develop facts before applying the law to arrive at legal conclusions or options; cite authorities as required; upholds professional responsibilities to the client and legal community. • Timely—deliver advice and counsel on-demand; anticipate issues and obstacles to mission completion; be proactive to prevent problems; meet timelines to support critical agency operations. Producing Substantive Advice in Crisis (SOAP) • Sense-making o Identify which values (and for whom) are at stake for the situation; o What are the critical uncertainties in the situation; o What is the time frame for developing and delivering advice; • Options o What authority allows a specific action; o What are we prohibited from doing; o What are the legal risks associated with the action; (ethical, political, etc.) o Is there a better way to achieve the goals; • Assessment o Authorization—Does the option appear to be authorized by statute or authority; o Prohibition—Is there a specific legal or policy-based prohibition, and where does it come from;	E, F, I, J		

Tasks	Code	Evaluation Record #	Evaluator Initials and Date
o Risk—what are the legal risks associated with the options;			
o Judgement—apply both practical and ethical judgement to the issue in question; is this for the greater good of this situation;			
• Provision of Advice			
o Adapting and packing advice in ways that are appropriate to the situation and the context in which the advice is being delivered.			
o Situational awareness—is the work under crisis-like conditions; time frames involved; pressure on the teams and leaders;			
o Organizational context—what is the nature of the organization (headquarters, regional office, Joint Field Office (JFO), ICP) and the culture;			
o Venue and form—what is the most appropriate way to convey the advice to a leader or other client (one-on-one meeting, at senior staff meeting, all-hands meeting, local officials meetings)			
o Risk picture—Whether to package the advice in terms of alternative levels of risk associated with an option (or) a go/no-go course of action; if risk level too high, does the leader want their lawyers to be prepared to express their objections;			
o Leader/collaborator personalities—cultivate the ability to adapt to the personalities and leadership styles of their clients;			
Mission Preparation and Readiness (PREP) for deployment:			
• Personal Commitment and Contact			
o Prepare for availability and extended absence;			
o Establish pre-departure communications with relevant agencies and partners;			
o Meet and greet with the appropriate city attorney (or legal representative), command staff, and other appropriate team members;			

Tasks	Code	Evaluation Record #	Evaluator Initials and Date
• Have a clear understanding of the ethical duties and the limits of personal knowledge of the law and professional development before providing legal advice in a crisis situation. • Reconnaissance (Mission) o Inform on the situation, context and role the attorney will be assuming; review declaration, Incident Management Assistance (IMAT) reports, source intelligence, hazard types and historical/geographical/cultural or jurisdictional context. • Emergency/Disaster Legal References o Compile and research general and specialized legal resources (authorities, regulations, policies, guidelines, procedures) • Packing List for Field Deployments o Travel or absence preparations; field kits; personal items.	E, F, I, J		
5. Provide or arrange for legal advice relating to EOC activities. Contact List (Liaison Officer) of subject matter attorneys (Environmental, Health, Criminal)			

6. Provide guidance to senior leadership, Policy Group and EOC personnel on potential legal risk and liabilities:
a. Establish a working relationship, including external partners and subject matter experts.
b. Anticipate potential legal problems and facilitate their resolution.
    • Agency Liability—Official capacity
    • Personal Liability—*Ultra Vires* section of Disaster Handbook (waivers of immunity, scope of authority, gross negligence)			

Tasks	Code	Evaluation Record #	Evaluator Initials and Date
7. Coordinate with local, state, tribal, territorial and federal emergency management attorneys.	E, F, I, J		

8. In coordination with EOC leadership and local, state, tribal, territorial and federal officials, draft the following:
a. Proclamations
  • City of Houston, Basic Emergency Plan, Annex U Legal, Section 15 Exhibits
    o Proclamation Declaring a Local State of Disaster
b. Declarations
  • City of Houston, Basic Emergency Plan, Annex U Legal, Section 15 Exhibits
    o Request for a State of Emergency after a disaster occurs
    o Request for a State of Emergency when disaster is imminent
  • Texas Emergency Management Executive Guide:
    o Sample Disaster Declaration
    o Sample Request Emergency Declaration to the Governor
c. Emergency ordinances
  • City of Houston, Basic Emergency Plan, Annex U Legal, Section 15 Exhibits
    o City Ordinance Extending a Local State of Disaster
    o City Ordinance Terminating a Local State of Disaster
d. Other legal documents
  • City of Houston, Basic Emergency Plan, Annex U Legal, Section 15 Exhibits
    o Executive Order
    o Executive Order Terminating a Local State of Disaster
	E, F, I, J		